PIANO SOLO

STAR WARS
THE FORCE AWAKENS

ISBN 978-1-4950-5331-3

© 2015 & TM Lucasfilm Ltd. All Rights Reserved.

Utapau Music

DISTRIBUTED BY

HAL•LEONARD®
CORPORATION

7777 W. BLUEMOUND RD. P.O. BOX 13819 MILWAUKEE, WI 53213

In Australia Contact:
Hal Leonard Australia Pty. Ltd.
4 Lentara Court
Cheltenham, Victoria, 3192 Australia
Email: ausadmin@halleonard.com.au

Visit Hal Leonard Online at
www.halleonard.com

MAIN TITLE AND THE ATTACK ON THE JAKKU VILLAGE

Music by JOHN WILLIAMS

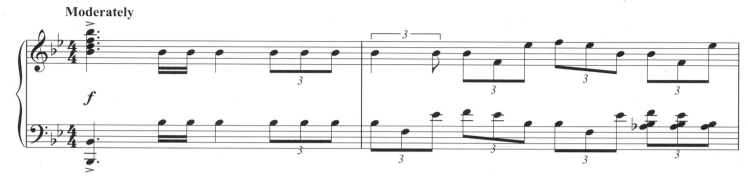

THE SCAVENGER

Music by JOHN WILLIAMS

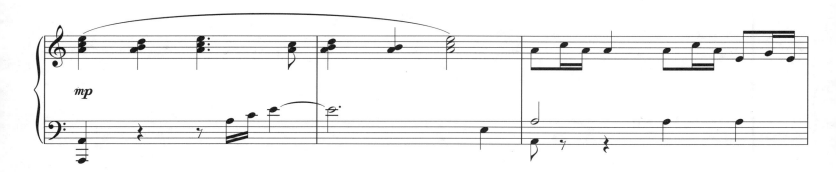

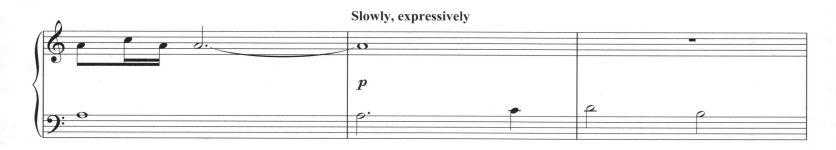

REY MEETS BB-8

Music by JOHN WILLIAMS

Slowly, in 2, expressively

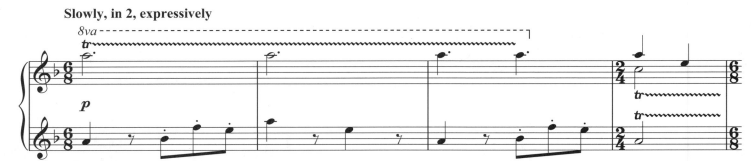

Pedal ad lib. throughout

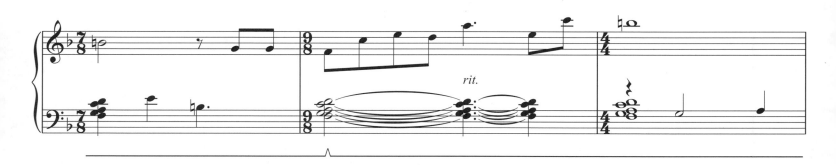

Moderately, with movement

REY'S THEME

Music by JOHN WILLIAMS

Moderately, steadily

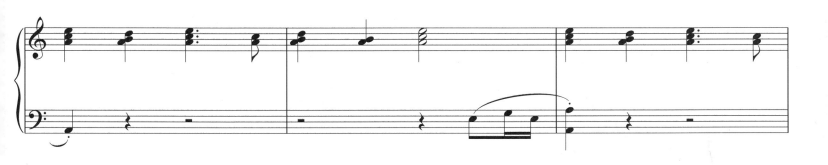

THAT GIRL WITH THE STAFF

Music by JOHN WILLIAMS

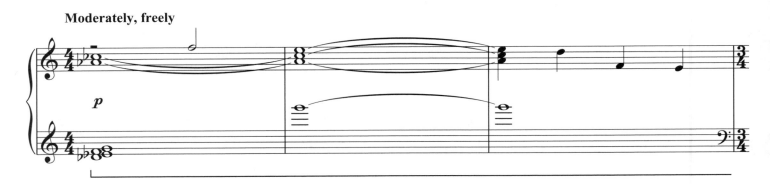

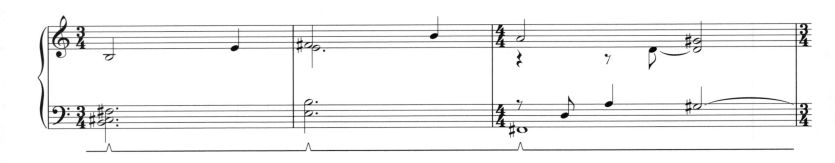

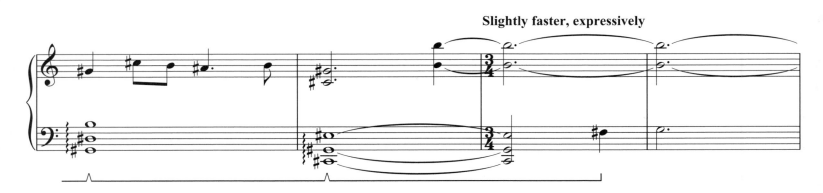

Moderately fast

FINN'S CONFESSION

Music by JOHN WILLIAMS

Moderately slow, expressively

mp

Pedal ad lib. throughout

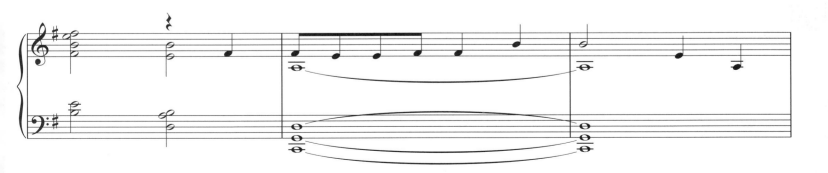

THE STARKILLER

Music by JOHN WILLIAMS

Moderately slow, expressively

Pedal ad lib. throughout

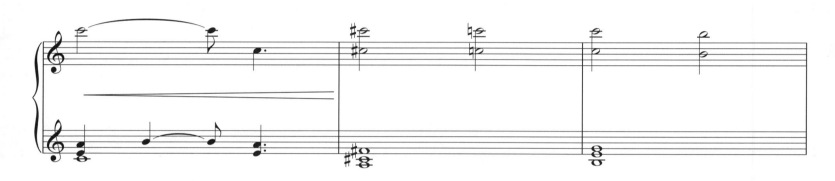

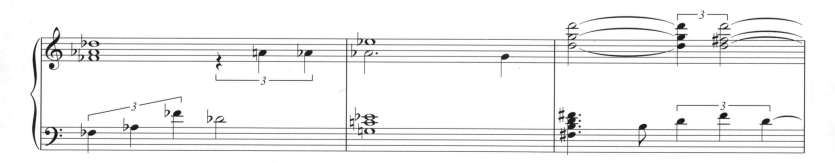

MARCH OF THE RESISTANCE

Music by JOHN WILLIAMS

SCHERZO FOR X-WINGS

Music by JOHN WILLIAMS

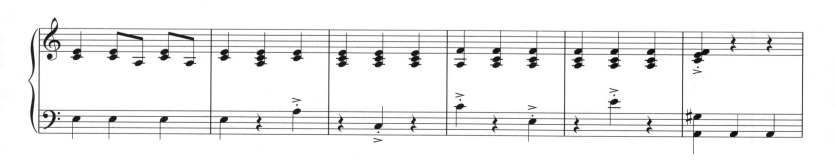

TORN APART

Music by JOHN WILLIAMS

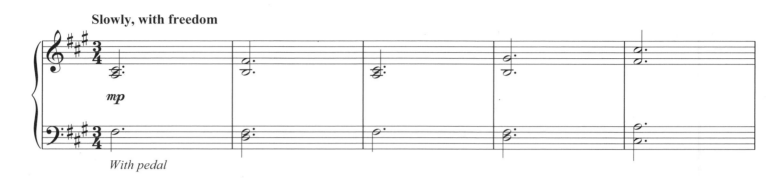

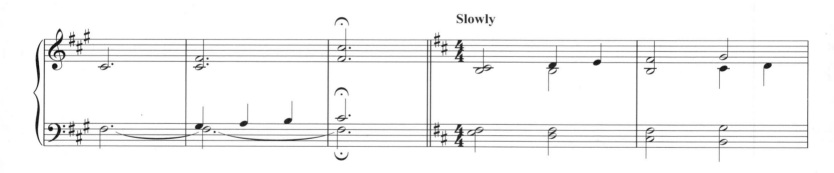

Quickly

FAREWELL AND THE TRIP

Music by JOHN WILLIAMS

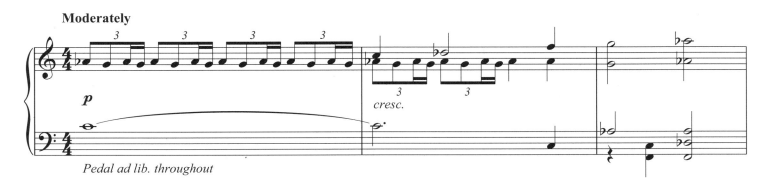

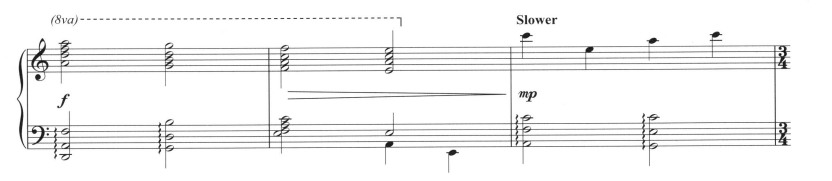

Moderately slow, expressively

Moderately fast, steadily

THE JEDI STEPS AND FINALE

Music by JOHN WILLIAMS

Moderately slow

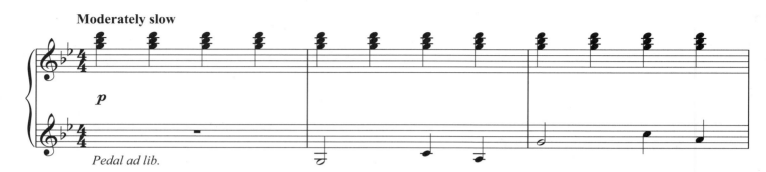

Pedal ad lib.

Moderately slow, expressively